The Unstoppables

Written by Samantha Montgomerie
Illustrated by Rebecca Burgess

Collins

1 Goal!

Mathilda keeps her eye on the ball and runs. There are only two minutes left of the game. Mathilda knows every second counts. Her heart is pounding. It is the semi-finals of the Junior Football Fever Tournament, and The Mighty Titans need just one more goal to win.

Mia dribbles the ball down the field towards the goal. The defence player who is marking her is closing in. She is going to steal the ball from Mia!

"I'm here!" calls Mathilda. She waves her arm to show Mia she is free.

Mia kicks and the ball shoots over to Mathilda.

Mathilda guides the ball with her feet and charges towards the goal. She can see the defence close beside her. Mathilda runs as fast as she can, fixing her eyes on the goal. She sees a spot just clear of the goalie. Mathilda kicks as hard as she can.

The ball flies into the net.

"Goal!" cries Coach Williams from the sideline.

The referee blows the whistle. "Game over," calls the referee.

A cheer erupts from the crowd. The Mighty Titans have won!

Mia races over and pats Mathilda on the back. "You did it!" pants Mia.

"We did it together!" replies Mathilda.

The team members flood around Mia and Mathilda. They laugh and whoop.

"Great goal!" says Lucy. She squeezes Mathilda in a tight hug. Mathilda grins.

"We're going to the finals!" beams Ivy, raising her hands in the air. The Mighty Titans cheer loudly.

"Great teamwork out there," says Coach Williams. "Now we have a week to prepare for the finals."

"We get a chance at being the season champs!" exclaims Mia.

"We certainly do!" says Coach Williams. "We'll be playing against The Hot Shots in the final."

"Oh no!" says Lucy. "The Hot Shots have been unbeaten for the last two years."

Coach Williams nods. "We're going to have to increase our training to topple them."

Mathilda feels her stomach knot. What if she isn't ready to play in the final? It will be a challenge to train that much. She has only just returned to football after her recent diagnosis of type 1 diabetes. What if she can't keep up? What if she stops them from winning the title?

2 The Unstoppables

Lucy has just arrived at Mathilda's house for a catch up. She bursts into Mathilda's room.

"Jade can't play!" cries Lucy. "She has sprained her ankle. Coach Williams wants me to be goalie!"

Lucy flops onto a bean bag and frowns. "I haven't played goalie since last year. What if I muck up and let the ball into the goal?"

"I'm worried I'll let the team down, too," says Mathilda. "What if my blood sugar levels get too low and I have to stop playing?"

"What we need is a plan so we're as ready as we can be," declares Lucy.

"Great idea!" says Mathilda as she grabs her pen and notebook. "We love football – we can't let this stop us enjoying the game!"

"That's it!" says Lucy. "From now on, we will call ourselves The Unstoppables."

Mathilda grins. She writes 'The Unstoppables' in the notebook and surrounds it with stars. She writes a big number 1 underneath it.

"Step one – stop worrying!" says Mathilda.

For the rest of the day, The Unstoppables set their plan into action.

"Step two – goalie practice!" declares Lucy.

Lucy stands in the goal. "Ready!" she says.

Mathilda kicks the ball hard. Lucy dives to block the ball from going in the goal.

"Perfect!" shouts Mathilda.

Lucy throws the ball back. "Again!" calls Lucy.

Mathilda puts a tick beside step two.

"Now for step three," says Lucy. "A food plan to manage blood sugar levels."

"Let's find Mum. It's time to count the carbs I just had for lunch," says Mathilda.

"Fabulous work," says Mum.

Mathilda grins at the food chart.

Mum opens an app on her phone. "Your blood sugar levels are looking great!"

Mathilda loves how her CGM monitor sends information to Mum's phone. Carbs are a great source of energy, but they also raise blood sugar levels. The CGM monitor helps Mathilda track the carbs she eats so that she can keep her blood sugars at the right level.

"Now, let's go into the activity mode and make an adjustment," says Mum. "This will change your insulin level while you're training more often."

"Let's get back out there," says Mathilda as she grabs the football.

"Nothing can stop us now!" exclaims Lucy.

3 Locked in!

Mathilda peers into her sports bag. She has her water bottle, snacks and her packet of emergency jellybeans in case she has a sugar low. She tucks her insulin pump into her belt. Mum has adjusted the activity mode. It's the day of the big game and Mathilda is ready to play!

"Who's ready to be named season champs?" asks Coach Williams.

"We are!" cheer the Mighty Titans.

Mathilda pats Lucy on the back. "Time to put our practice into action," says Mathilda.

Mathilda and Lucy have been preparing all week.

"Let's show them what The Unstoppables can do!" declares Lucy.

"Make sure you have everything you need for the game. There are 15 minutes before we're on!" states Coach Williams.

"I need my gloves!" says Lucy.

"And I need my tournament shirt," cries Mathilda.

Lucy and Mathilda sprint over to the clubhouse.

"Hey!" says Lucy. "Our tournament shirts have gone!"

"Where are they?" asks Lucy.

Mathilda hears a laugh. She looks up to see Alice and Amy, players from The Hot Shots, watching them. They sneer as they watch Lucy race behind the club shed in search of the shirts.

"Found them!" cries Lucy. She races back clutching the shirts. "Someone had hidden all of them!"

Mathilda glares at Amy and Alice, who are whispering and giggling together as they spy Lucy with the shirts.

"I think I know who that someone might be," says Mathilda. "And I think I might just tell them what I think of their rotten joke!"

"No," says Lucy. She tugs at Mathilda's arm. "We don't have time. We need to get changed as fast as we can, or we will be subbed off for the start."

Mathilda gives Amy and Alice a steely glare before turning to follow Lucy into the changing room.

4 A hopeful dash

"Quick," says Lucy, giving Mathilda her tournament shirt.

"The Hot Shots are trying to make us late so they can win!" declares Mathilda.

"Well, we're going to show them their nasty plan didn't work!" exclaims Lucy.

They rush to change into their gear.

A door slams. There is a loud click. Mathilda races to the door and gives it a tug. Her heart sinks.

"They've locked us in!" cries Mathilda.

Mathilda pulls on the door handle, but it will not budge.

They hear the whistle blow. "Oh no, the game's going to start without us!" cries Mathilda.

"Look!" says Lucy. She points up at an open window. "That might be our way out!"

Mathilda peers up at the window. "Maybe I can get out through there?"

"Use your hands to hoist me up," says Lucy.

Mathilda links her fingers together and holds them low. Lucy places her foot in Mathilda's hands.

"Ready?" asks Mathilda.

"Ready!" says Lucy.

Mathilda lifts her hands up as Lucy pushes off with her other foot, hoisting Lucy up to the windowsill.

Clutching the windowsill, Lucy wiggles and pulls herself up. She grins at Mathilda.

"Almost there!" says Lucy. She peers out of the window. "It's not far to drop down."

She swivels around so that her legs dangle towards the ground. She gives one final grin as she eases herself down the other side.

Mathilda waits for the door to click. It swings open. Lucy is there, grinning widely.

"We did it!" says Lucy. "Now, let's get to the pitch – we have a game to play!"

They sprint off.

"Where have you been?" asks Coach Williams.

Mathilda tells her about being locked in.
Coach Williams rushes to tell the referee. The referee stops the game.

"Due to cheating by The Hot Shots, The Mighty Titans have won," says the referee.

"It's a shame the actions of two people ruin it for all of us," sighs Mathilda.

"Let me talk to the ref," says Coach Williams.

Coach Williams asks the referee if The Mighty Titans could have a chance to win that is fair. The referee grins. "Well, let's get on with the game then! But first, Amy and Alice need to sit on the sideline."

Setting her eye on the goal, Mathilda makes a run for it. There is only one minute left in the game. Every second counts. Mathilda drives the ball close to the goal and lines it up. She kicks. The crowd holds its breath …

"Goal!" cries Coach Williams. The whistle blows. The Mighty Titans have won! The team cheers and races to celebrate Mathilda for her winning goal.

"I guess we really are unstoppable after all," says Lucy, smiling.

The Unstoppables

1. Stop worrying

2. Goalie practice

3. Monitor blood sugar levels

4. Pack emergency jellybeans ✓

5. Play hard! ✓

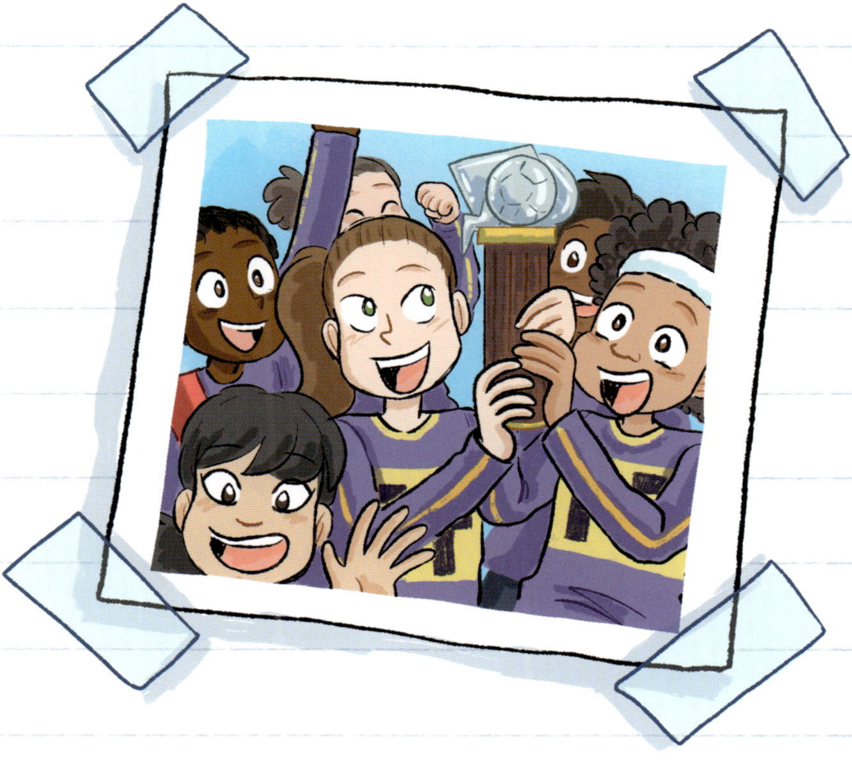

Ideas for reading

Written by Gill Matthews
Primary Literacy Consultant

Reading objectives:
- make inferences on the basis of what is being said and done
- answer and ask questions
- predict what might happen on the basis of what has been read so far

Spoken language objectives:
- articulate and justify answers, arguments and opinions
- use spoken language to develop understanding through speculating, hypothesising, imagining and exploring ideas
- participate in discussions, presentations, performances, role play, improvisations and debates

Curriculum links: Relationships education: Caring friendships
Interest words: calls, cries, pants, beams, exclaims
Word count: 1543

Build a context for reading
- Ask children to look at the front cover of the book and to read the title.
- Discuss what the title means to them.
- Read the back cover blurb. Explore what children think might happen in the book.

Understand and apply reading strategies
- Read pp2–8 aloud, using meaning, dialogue and punctuation to help you to read with appropriate expression.
- Discuss what children have found out from this first chapter.
- Explore what first impressions they have of the characters.
- Ask children to read pp9–15 quietly to themselves, focussing on reading with appropriate expression.